NATIONAL GEOGRAPHIC

Common Core Readers

Ladders

Catch the Light

BRIGHT LIGHTS HAVE A DARK SIDE

by Jennifer Boudart

A view of the United States at night reveals a dot-to-dot pattern of lights from coast to coast. To the average eye, the lights seem beautiful, even comforting. However, a growing number of scientists find the view troubling. Yet the value of artificial light to the human race cannot be overstated.

2

When Thomas Edison introduced the first practical light bulb in the late 1800s, it changed the way we spent our time. Life became safer and more productive after dark, both indoors and out. Today we link to an electric grid, which can light a room, a street corner, or an entire city.

Is all that night light too much of a good thing? People studying the effects of artificial light call it light pollution, and they claim it's potentially hurting not only the environment but human health, too.

This satellite image of the United States shows how much light shines at night.

There is growing evidence that light pollution in place of natural darkness is more than just a loss of stargazing. In fact, it's changing the very rhythm of life on Earth, including the daily rhythms of human activity.

Pollution happens when a harmful substance enters the environment. Pollution can poison the air, land, and water, or threaten plant and animal life. In many places, night is no longer truly night, as a result of light pollution and its effects. Light pollution's effects take the form of sky glow, light trespass, and **glare.**

In the U. S., street lighting is less than 1% of electricity use. Yet there are plenty of street and alley lights in all cities.

70,000	Ann Arbor, MI
118,000	Philadelphia, PA
250,000	Chicago, IL
300,000	New York, NY

TOO MUCH LIGHT

People seem compelled to push back the night. They light their homes and yards. They light office buildings long after the workday ends. They light empty parking lots in strip malls and car dealerships. Often lights stay on all night long. They over illuminate, or give off much more light than is really needed. They also produce a harsh glare, instead of a gentle glow, and many lights are poorly designed for their purpose. They send too much light where it is *not* needed and not enough where it *is* needed.

Light shining up from the ground creates a glow—sky glow. It makes the night sky look bright when the sky is naturally mostly dark. Some sources of sky glow are natural, including small amounts of sunlight, moonlight, and starlight bouncing off Earth. But most sky glow is because of outdoor electric light. Examples of outdoor lights that create sky glow include streetlights, billboards, mounted lights on buildings, interior lights shining through windows, and lights over ball fields and other public spaces.

All this electric light creates a glowing dome over cities and towns. The glow over a populated area may be seen for hundreds of miles! Night sky objects, like stars and planets, are less visible. Nowadays city dwellers looking up at the night sky are unlikely to see any stars or other natural features of the night sky.

Light trespass is another form of light pollution. Trespass—also known as spill light—happens when ground-level light sources shine light into places where it isn't wanted. For example, a homeowner may turn on lights over his or her garage for security, and those lights shine into the windows of nearby houses, bothering people who live there. Lights also shine into homes from nearby office parks, shopping centers, and other buildings that are kept illuminated at night.

Glare, unshielded light shining straight out from its source, can be dangerous because it interferes with the ability to see in the dark. When a person's eyes encounter a flash of bright light, the light fills his or her entire field of view. The person will then have a hard time detecting obstacles while the eyes adjust. Groups of bright lights may also confuse a person. The lights may distract him or her from obstacles, which can cause accidents.

Glare is especially hazardous for older people attempting to walk or drive at night. Like other forms of light pollution, glare results from streetlights, parking lot lights, field lighting, and other stationary lights. Moving vehicle lights can also cause glare.

The same lights that contribute to sky glow also contribute to light trespass. Homeowners may not realize the impact that exterior lights can have on people living nearby. Unless people put dark shades over their windows, they're bound to experience some trespass light shining into their homes.

Most billboards are lit from below, and the light shines up from fixtures mounted along the billboard's bottom. Most of that light escapes into the night sky. If billboard lights were positioned on top of the billboard, light could be directed downward, thus reducing light pollution.

5

SOME LAWS TARGET LIGHT POLLUTION BY

- setting light curfews

- limiting light bulb brightness

- banning lights of a certain color

INDIVIDUALS CAN ALSO HELP BY

- using motion sensor lights

- buying light fixtures with shields to better direct light

- installing timer controls and dimmers

Light emits both day and night from buildings in large cities like Chicago, Illinois. The light of the night sky is barely visible until one travels many miles outside of the city.

HEALTH AND WELL-BEING

People might say that light pollution is just the price we pay for being able to see at night. Some might claim that light pollution should only concern astronomers and stargazers, and observatories certainly are plagued by problems with light pollution. Even a 10 percent increase in sky glow above natural levels makes telescopes less effective. But that is only a more obvious part of the problem. In our modern world, light pollution is also taking a toll on our health and well-being.

In the past, ancient people looked to the stars to guide their travels. They told stories about the night sky. However, in just over a century, since the invention of electric light, humans have turned away from the stars and for many, the night sky has become downright alien.

In 1994, an earthquake knocked out power in Los Angeles. As darkness engulfed the city, calls began flooding local 911 centers. People reported seeing a strange silvery cloud in the sky. They made anxious phone calls because they worried what they saw was related to the earthquake. In fact, it was the Milky Way. These people had either never seen it or couldn't identify it.

The human body is programmed to respond to natural patterns of daylight and darkness. We are adapted to be **diurnal** creatures, mostly active during the day and at rest after dark. Many of our bodily functions, from brain wave patterns to cell activity, follow a predictable pattern every 24 hours or so. This is in keeping with periods of day and night, but those periods are changing.

Artificial light enables us to ignore our body rhythms and push activity later and later into the wee hours. Unlike some animals that are most active at night, humans are not **nocturnal**. Before electric lights became common, people slept an average of eight hours a night. Today adults in America average a bit fewer than seven hours of sleep most nights. While that isn't a large difference in the amount of sleep, the real difference is the number of hours people can stay active because of artificial light. Previously, people were active only during hours of natural daylight, 10 to 14 hours depending on the season. Now 15.5 million people in the United States work night shifts and sleep during the day.

Americans are also finding it harder to fall asleep, and research shows that artificial light suppresses the release of a hormone called *melatonin*. This is the hormone that makes us feel sleepy and regulates our sleep/wake cycle.

Too much light at night can affect the natural rhythms and patterns of animal life.

Sea turtles struggle to find dark beaches needed for egg laying. When the eggs hatch, baby turtles look for light reflecting off the water to find the sea. They can become confused by beachfront lights and crawl the wrong way.

Large metropolitan areas glow with lights from buildings, streetlights, and homes. Medical research has started to show how extra exposure to artificial light may be connected to sleep problems, obesity, and even some forms of cancer.

The Milky Way as seen from
South Island, New Zealand.

26,000 LIGHT YEARS
distance from Earth to the center of the Milky Way

100 BILLION
stars in the Milky Way

13 BILLION YEARS
age of the oldest stars in the galaxy

OUR GALAXY

Earth and its solar system are part of the Milky Way Galaxy. From Earth, the center of the Milky Way is about 26,000 light years away. Interstellar dust (star dust) blocks clear telescope views of much of the Milky Way.

The Milky Way includes about 100 billion stars, maybe more. The oldest stars are in the middle of the galaxy. Such stars may be around 13 billion years old.

LIGHT POLLUTION SOLUTIONS

There is a growing movement around the world to reduce light pollution. The International Dark-Sky Association (IDA) is one of the movement's leaders. IDA works with like-minded groups to raise public awareness and reduce light pollution through "environmentally responsible outdoor lighting." IDA describes the night sky as "one half of the entire planet's natural environment" and says it should be considered a natural resource.

IDA has established the International Dark Sky Places program, which identifies International Dark Sky communities, parks, and reserves. To receive this recognition, sites must not only be free of light pollution, but additionally, landowners, cities, or towns must also allow public access to these sites and run public education programs.

It's easy to ignore the beauty of the night sky when we cannot truly see it. Only a few dozen stars shine through sky glow above a city or town. But on a truly dark night, in a truly dark place, as many as 7,000 stars shine overhead and so does the Milky Way. Turn off the lights and head into the night. It's out there, waiting for you!

Natural Bridges National Monument is in Utah. It is the world's first International Dark Sky Park.

The Light Catchers

by Allan Woodrow
illustrated by Tuesday Mourning

The sky was dark, middle-of-the-night dark, even though it was only two hours past lunchtime. Why did they have to spend winter vacation with Grandpa Saul, anyway? If anyone asked Trevor for his opinion, he would have suggested they travel someplace far warmer, far brighter, and far closer. Nine-year old Trevor and his eleven-year-old sister, Alice, flew on a plane for 13 hours to get all the way to their destination of Barrow, Alaska. Barrow's claim to fame is that it's the northernmost city in the United States. That, and this interesting fact: this time of year it is dark 24-hours a day.

Barrow, being so far north and so close to the North Pole, doesn't have regular days and nights, or at least not all year long. During the winter in Barrow, the sun sets in mid-November and doesn't rise again until the end of January. This made a visit to Barrow during these few months more of a **nocturnal** experience.

Just as odd, during the summer, Barrow goes almost three months without a sunset. To Trevor, playing outside all night long in daylight sounded a lot more exhilarating than being stuck in an endless night.

White, icy precipitation fell outside, a snow blizzard really, with cold, gusty winds so strong Trevor expected them to lift the house and toss it away. It was bitterly icy cold, too, fitting Barrow's reputation, as it was below freezing most of the year, and it could snow anytime, even in July.

Making matters worse, Grandpa didn't like to keep too many lights on; he constantly preached how energy conservation was essential to life in this rural area. He didn't even like to operate the dishwasher! But Trevor would have been much more content if every light in the house blared all day long; he despised the dark. Unfamiliar things lurked in the blackness that didn't lurk during the day, and in the dark, anything could happen.

Trevor was pondering those exact thoughts when the unthinkable happened right there and then—the electricity went out and, naturally, all the lights with it, creating a total **blackout.**

Trevor tensed, and his sense of hearing became more acute. He was certain a creature was in the room, a particularly devious creature, probably under the bed or in the closet, and he heard footsteps out in the hall creaking on the hardwood floor. He sensed something entering the room coming to get him, and he screamed.

"What's wrong?" gasped Alice, Trevor's older sister.

Trevor held on to something fleshy and bony. "I'm holding a monster!" he cried.

"You're holding my arm," said Alice, "Let go, you're hurting me!" She flipped her flashlight switch and shone the ray at Trevor, who was quivering while grasping Alice's arm in a death-like grip.

"Sorry," Trevor said, releasing his hold.

"Let's go downstairs. Grandpa told me to come get you," grumbled Alice, shaking her arm. "Get a hold of yourself. "

"If you don't want to be treated like a monster, you shouldn't sneak into my room like one," scowled Trevor.

"I wasn't sneaking, and why haven't you unpacked your suitcase?" asked Alice.

"I'll do it later, and there's no need to act like Mom, you know. Besides, it's fifteen degrees below outside and not much warmer in here. I feel like I should wear layers of everything I brought," said Trevor, rolling his eyes.

Downstairs, Grandpa Saul waited patiently on the floor of the family room. He sat so motionlessly Trevor didn't see him at first, not until Alice's flashlight illuminated him. In the dark, Grandpa's wrinkles looked like small canyons and his smile, normally bright and cheerful, looked almost mischievous. Alice and Trevor sat on the floor next to him.

"Don't worry, these blackouts don't last long, and I expect the lights should turn on soon enough," said Grandpa Saul.

"Blackouts are usually caused by faulty **infrastructure**, otherwise known as The Grid," said Alice confidently. "Much of the grid is comprised of old power plants and power lines that need to be upgraded."

Grandpa appreciated and admired his granddaughter's love of scientific facts, but he brushed it off and snorted, "Ha! It's the Light Catchers' fault. You've heard of the Light Catchers, right?"

"I'm not in the mood for ghost stories, Grandpa," said Trevor, shaking his head. His grandpa loved telling fanciful tall tales with exceedingly good details, which sometimes were gruesome, and sometimes comical.

"Please tell us, Grandpa," exclaimed Alice who loved fanciful tales as much as scientific facts. "I want to hear the story. Trevor is just a scaredy-cat."

"I am not a scaredy-cat! Go ahead, Grandpa, I want to hear the story, too," Trevor said, unconvincingly.

Grandpa Saul took Alice's flashlight and held it below his chin so the beam lit up his face. The stream of eerie, yellow-green light made grandpa look positively frightening.

"Those pixie Light Catchers are scary things, only a few inches tall, but angry and spiteful. They look like little, unpleasant people, except with dragonfly wings and long stingers instead of noses. They steal the lights from the porches or street lamps and eat light. You see, it tastes like cupcakes to them. They suck a ball of light into their stingers and bring it home for their babies to eat."

"Cool! Do you think we can locate a Light Catcher if we go outside to hunt for one?" Alice asked eagerly.

Her grandfather shook his head. "They're nocturnal, so they only come out at night, and mostly avoid people if they can, sort of pixie recluses. But back when I was a young man they were much bolder, buzzing around by the dozens like giant, mean-spirited hornets, chasing people and gobbling up light. It got so unbearable people went right to sleep when it got dark because they knew their light would be sucked up by the Light Catchers, anyway."

"Electric light is a valuable commodity around here," Grandpa said, "as valuable as water or food. I couldn't have these little pests stealing it all the time, so I decided to catch one. In those days, there was a barn in the back of the house. One night, I left a candle glowing on a window ledge and nimbly hid behind a big pickle barrel. When one of those Light Catchers came for a nibble of light, I jumped out holding a glass jar, scooped up that little fellow and popped on the lid. After Light Catchers eat, they glow like the brightest fireflies you've ever seen. That bright, shining Light Catcher was so infuriated, he spat and cursed and shook his tiny fist at me, but I just laughed and put the jar in the barn for safekeeping. 'That'll teach you to tamper with my lights,' I told him, and the pixie just snarled back at me."

"The next evening, those nocturnal, night-loving pixies came, a whole horde of them, swooping and crashing into the house, stealing all the lights from a mile around. I grabbed a big butterfly net and spent the entire night chasing those angry creatures everywhere. They were fast and slippery, but after a few hours I captured about a hundred and put them in jars in the barn. You should have seen that barn glow! You could see it clear across Barrow."

"Too bad they can't use some of those pixies at the power plant," said Alice, "Think about all the energy conservation we'd have then! With all their light, there would never be blackouts."

Grandpa shook his head and said, "You should never catch a Light Catcher, as I was about to find that out the hard way."

"The pixies were enraged," continued Grandpa, making an angry face. The flashlight made his expression look menacing, and Trevor gulped in fright. "I couldn't get near the barn without hearing the Light Catchers yelling and screaming like crazy. Pixies don't like to be confined or cooped up; they like their freedom, just like you and me. I was terrified to release them; I didn't know what they'd do and I was concerned it wasn't going to be nice. But I thought and thought, and I decided that I couldn't keep them trapped any longer; it was just plain mean and I wasn't vindictive. So I went to the barn the next night to let them out."

"I should have been paying attention to the weather forecast; I didn't realize a big storm had been blowing in all day. As soon as I approached the barn, I heard the wind howling and saw the shutters of the barn shaking. I had never witnessed a storm like that; it was almost like a hurricane! The intensity of the storm uprooted a giant oak tree that nearly smashed into the house. The barn swayed, too, and the doors violently crashed open and then, just like that, the walls blew away."

"Were the pixies injured?" asked Alice, leaning closer to her grandfather. "Tell me they were OK!"

"It's just a make-believe story," said Trevor with a laugh, but then he added quietly, "They were OK, right, Grandpa?"

"You bet they were OK," said Grandpa Saul. "Unfortunately. The Light Catchers weren't hurt at all, but the wind shattered all their jars, and the pixies were no longer captive. They were free as birds, very irate birds. They were out to get me, buzzing around and charging at me with their stingers. I ran back inside the house to escape their pursuit, but they were hot on my tail. I barely made it back inside in one piece!"

"I could see the pixies outside, devouring the lights all around. They weren't just hungry; they wanted revenge. They consumed all the lights around the house and in town. The next day, the newspaper reported high winds had knocked down some power lines, and the infrastructure had been torn to pieces, but I knew the truth. It was the pixies."

"But they didn't stop there, not those crazed, angry imps. They were still raving mad and apparently still ravenously hungry, and a few of them flew all the way up to the sun, thousands of millions of miles up into the sky. They greedily gorged on the sun's light, feasting on the rays and stashing them inside their pointy stingers, plunging all of Barrow into darkness.

"It took weeks for the sun to grow brightly again, and now, once a year, the grudge-holding pixies fly back up to the sun and steal the light, keeping it for two months, all because of what I did. That's the reason it's dark for so long every winter in Barrow, just because of those light-loving nocturnal pests. And that's why you should be warned—never try to catch a Light Catcher."

"That's the silliest story I've ever heard," said Trevor. Grandpa Saul merely shrugged.

A static charge filled the room, a ZZZZPPPT, and all the lights popped back on, bathing the house in bright illumination once more. "Looks like the 'ole power grid is working again," Grandpa said.

Trevor looked out the window into the darkness, and saw something glowing outside. Trevor squinted to get a better look at a nasty, winged creature with a long stinger staring in at him. But it couldn't be … could it?

"Is that a …" said Trevor, but as soon as he pointed at the creature, it turned and flew away, if it had even been there at all. Trevor shook his head, figuring it must have been his way-too, overactive imagination—maybe.

Check In How did Grandpa Saul explain Alaska's seasonal light and dark periods?

Daylight Saving Time— PRO or CON?

by Jennifer Boudart

"Spring forward, fall back." This familiar phrase reminds us to change our clocks twice each year, in keeping with Daylight Saving Time (DST). The United States first implemented DST nearly 100 years ago to maximize daylight hours in summer and to conserve energy. Many people appreciate DST, but others claim it is ineffective and want to **abolish** it.

Life is better with Daylight Saving Time. Daylight Saving Time improves our health. When DST goes into effect, television watching drops and outdoor recreation increases. This is beneficial to family relationships and health because being outside playing together is a better use of family time than watching movies.

DST makes us safer. When DST is in effect, people can travel home from work and school before dark, when driving conditions are safer. A study published in 2007 showed that, in the last 30 years, traffic accidents fell six to ten percent during DST months. Crime rates fell, too.

DST saves energy. The average home spends a quarter of its energy budget to power appliances and lights in the evening. Extended daylight reduces this type of energy use. In fact, studies show that on a national level, DST saves us enough energy each year to power about 100,000 households.

DST helps the environment. By reducing energy use, DST reduces pollution. More than half our nation's electricity comes from burning coal, which produces ugly smog and acid rain. Turning lights on later means fewer hours of artificial light. This reduction in light pollution improves the quality of life for **nocturnal** wildlife.

DST boosts the economy. Certain industries see profits rise when DST goes into effect. For example, golf courses, recreation areas, and many stores extend their hours during DST and thus enjoy more profits from customers.

These reasons support the continuance of Daylight Saving Time in the United States. Through this practice we help our society in several ways.

CON

Life is not better with Daylight Saving Time. Did you know our government does not even **mandate** DST?

DST threatens our health. Health experts claim our internal body clocks—set by light and darkness—never adjust to gaining an extra hour of daylight. The change makes it more difficult for people to fall asleep. As a result, people sleep less and get sick more. Is saving a bit of energy worth our health?

Proponents of DST claim that extending daylight improves driving safety. The reality is that people easily adjust to less light in the evenings with the winter season. DST extends daylight by one hour.

However, in winter, the sun sets before most people can drive home from work. People regularly work more than nine hours a day, which means that their morning or evening commute (or both) still take place when it's dark. DST can increase energy use. It's true DST saves energy on the national level,

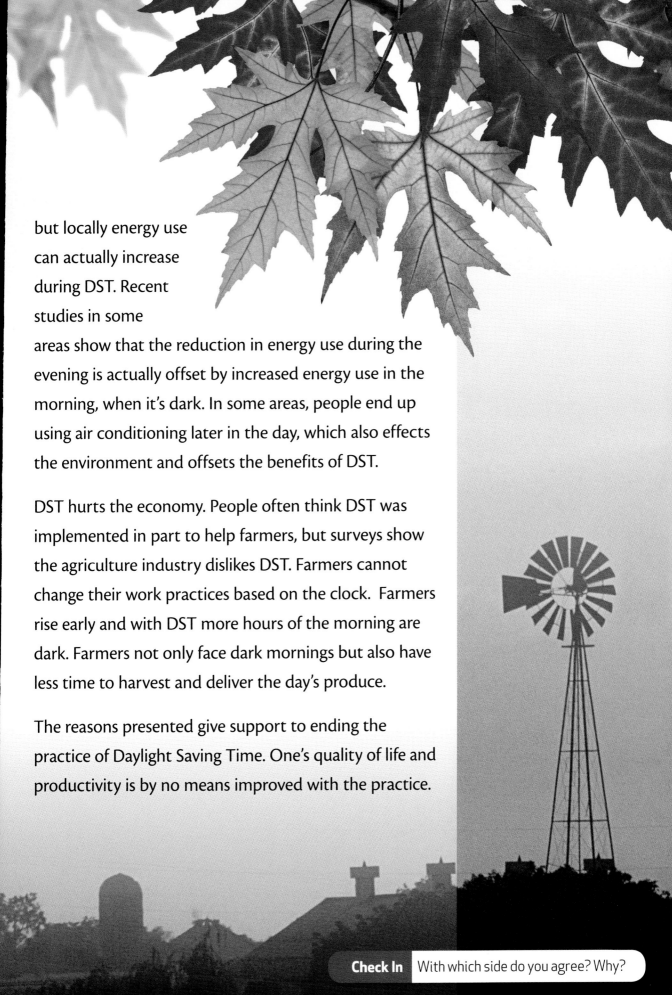

but locally energy use can actually increase during DST. Recent studies in some areas show that the reduction in energy use during the evening is actually offset by increased energy use in the morning, when it's dark. In some areas, people end up using air conditioning later in the day, which also effects the environment and offsets the benefits of DST.

DST hurts the economy. People often think DST was implemented in part to help farmers, but surveys show the agriculture industry dislikes DST. Farmers cannot change their work practices based on the clock. Farmers rise early and with DST more hours of the morning are dark. Farmers not only face dark mornings but also have less time to harvest and deliver the day's produce.

The reasons presented give support to ending the practice of Daylight Saving Time. One's quality of life and productivity is by no means improved with the practice.

Check In With which side do you agree? Why?

1. What connections can you make among the three pieces in *Catch the Light*? How are the pieces related?

2. Compare the information you learned in the science article, "Bright Lights Have a Dark Side," with the information you learned in the opinion piece. How is the information alike and different?

3. What is the relationship between artificial light and light pollution?

4. What did you visualize when Grandpa Saul told his story about the Light Catchers? Did the illustrations match the picture in your mind?

5. What reasons and evidence were most persuasive in the opinion piece? Did you change your opinion after reading both sides, pro and con? Why or why not?

6. What questions do you still have about the natural and artificial light?